Acknowledgments

Nihil Obstat

I have concluded that the materials presented in this work are free of doctrinal or moral errors.

Bernadeane Carr, STL
Censor Librorum, September 21, 1995

Imprimatur

In accord with 1983 CIC 827 #3, permission to publish this work is hereby granted.

+Robert H. Brom
Bishop of San Diego, October 4, 1995

Scripture selections are taken from or based upon the *New American Bible*,
Copyright © 1991, 1986, 1970
Confraternity of Christian Doctrine,
Washington, D.C. 20017
and are used with permission. All rights reserved.

Production

Game Design	Michael J. McKay, S.T.D.
Questions & Answers	Michael J. McKay, S.T.D. Rand Reichert, M. Div. Debbie Brumley
Graphic Design Illustration	Connie Boulton Tom Voss

Copyright © 1995 by Divinity Religious Products, Inc.

tio...
...can be asked in any order or from any page. Answers are given on the back of the page where the questions are found. Most answers are referenced to the paragraph number (par. #) of the *Catechism of the Catholic Church* or to the chapter and verse numbers of the *New American Bible*. Every page contains four color-coded questions corresponding to the major sections of the Catechism:

Blue Question	Believe (Profession of Faith)
Yellow Question	Celebrate (Sacraments)
Red Question	Live (Morality)
Purple Question	Pray (Christian Prayer)

Keeping Score

Points are scored for each correct answer. Point values are displayed under each answer (1, 2 or 3 points) with 3 points being the most difficult. The first player/team reaching a total of 10 points for each color category (40 points total), wins the game.

Catholic Challenge
Student Contest

Catholic Challenge is an exciting opportunity for elementary school kids to compete in a parish or school contest helping them to learn more about the important beliefs and traditions of the Catholic Faith.

Anyone can win and everyone who competes in the Catholic Challenge Contest will enjoy a new sense of confidence by learning more about their faith and religious values.

To find out more about the Catholic Challenge Contest call or write:

Divinity Religious Products, Inc.
5115 Avenida Encinas, Suite B
Carlsbad, CA 92008

1-800-669-9200
Fax: 1-760-929-0479

Become a Winner!

Everyone knows that kids love to play games. Now kids have a chance to become winners by answering grade level questions about their faith with Catholic Quiz flip books.

Ask your religion teacher about a locally and nationally organized "Religion Bee" called Catholic Challenge.

See reverse side for details.

Answers

False (par. 253-255)

(2 points)

(c) the flood waters (par. 1219)

(1 point)

(b) being reverent towards God

(2 points)

(c) their lack of faith (par. 2610)

(2 points)

Questions

God the Father is the most important person of the Blessed Trinity.
True or false?

What symbolizes Baptism in the story of Noah?
(a) the dove with the olive branch
(b) the rainbow
(c) the flood waters

What does "fear of the Lord" mean?
(a) being afraid of God
(b) being reverent towards God
(c) not taking the Lord's name in vain

What often saddened Jesus about his followers?
(a) their sin
(b) their arguments
(c) their lack of faith

Answers

False (par. 998)

(2 points)

(c) Jesus Christ (par. 1642)

(2 points)

(b) a child (par. 2378)

(1 point)

(c) constantly (par. 2633)

(2 points)

Questions

At the end of the world only the good will rise from the dead.
True or false?

Who is the source of grace in the sacrament of Matrimony?
(a) the couple
(b) the priest
(c) Jesus Christ

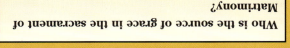

Which is the most important gift of marriage?
(a) companionship
(b) a child
(c) a home

St. James and St. Paul urge us to pray _____.
(a) daily
(b) weekly
(c) constantly

Answers

(c) Jesus (par. 505)

(1 point)

False (par. 1264)

(2 points)

(b) promises (par. 2101)

(1 point)

False (par. 2612)

(1 point)

Questions

Who is called the "New Adam?"
(a) John the Baptist
(b) Moses
(c) Jesus

Those who are baptized will never experience suffering or death.
True or false?

Some of the sacraments require us to make _____ to God.
(a) excuses
(b) promises
(c) financial offerings

Prayer cannot keep us from falling into temptation.
True or false?

Answers

False (par. 982)

(2 points)

True (par. 1641)

(1 point)

(b) work to avoid war (par. 2308)

(1 point)

False (par. 2665)

(2 points)

Questions

The Church cannot forgive all sins.
True or false?

Like all the sacraments, marriage has its own special grace.
True or false?

Nations should always _____.
(a) build up their defenses
(b) work to avoid war
(c) seek to be the strongest

Liturgical prayer in the Church is always addressed to the Father.
True or false?

Answers

(a) soul (par. 365)

(1 point)

False (par. 1261)

(2 points)

(a) prayer (par. 2098)

(1 point)

(b) the Psalter (par. 2587)

(2 points)

Questions

A human being is made up of body and _____.
(a) soul
(b) antibody
(c) blood

The Church teaches that children who die without being baptized will never go to heaven. True or false?

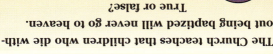

What is needed to obey God's commandments?
(a) prayer
(b) perfection
(c) fear

What prayer in the Old Testament are songs of God's saving works?
(a) the Song of Songs
(b) the Psalter
(c) the Beatitudes

Answers

(a) at Baptism (par. 978)

(3 points)

(b) marriage (par. 1609)

(2 points)

(c) stewards (par. 2280)

(2 points)

(c) a tiny whispering sound (1Kgs 19:11-13)

(2 points)

Questions

When do we make our first profession of faith in the Catholic Church?
(a) at Baptism
(b) at First Holy Communion
(c) at First Confession

What helps man and woman overcome the effects of sin in the world?
(a) riches
(b) marriage
(c) technology

God has made us _____ of our lives.
(a) masters
(b) slaves
(c) stewards

What caused Elijah to hide his face from God?
(a) fire
(b) earthquake
(c) a tiny whispering sound

Answers

False (par. 356)

(2 points)

(c) baptism (par. 1254)

(2 points)

(c) peace for all (par. 1909)

(2 points)

(c) how to be part of the coming kingdom (par. 2607)

(2 points)

Questions

All of God's creatures are able to know and love him.
True or false?

What promises are renewed at the Easter Vigil to strengthen faith?
(a) marriage
(b) ordination
(c) baptism

What will never happen without justice in our society?
(a) jobs for all
(b) food for all
(c) peace for all

About what did Jesus often speak in his parables?
(a) paying tribute to the State
(b) being submissive to the authorities
(c) how to be part of the coming kingdom

Answers

(b) John, the beloved disciple (Jn 19:25-27)

(2 points)

(b) celibacy (par. 1579)

(3 points)

False (par. 2173)

(1 point)

(c) a place for prayer (par. 2691)

(3 points)

Questions

Jesus gave the care of Mary, his mother, to _____.
(a) Lazarus
(b) John, the beloved disciple
(c) Elizabeth

The sign that priests serve the Lord with an "undivided heart" is called _____.
(a) poverty
(b) celibacy
(c) obedience

Jesus did not respect the Sabbath. True of false?

What is an oratory?
(a) a place for the priest to vest
(b) a place to practice homilies
(c) a place for prayer

Answers

(b) angels (par. 350)

(1 point)

(b) at the wedding in Cana (Jn 2:1-12)

(2 points)

(b) ignorance of God (par. 2087)

(3 points)

(c) to call people to a change of heart
    (par. 2595)

(2 points)

Questions

Who constantly give glory to God?
(a) priests
(b) angels
(c) prophets

Where did Jesus perform the first of his miracles?
(a) at his baptism
(b) at the wedding in Cana
(c) at the Transfiguration
(d) none of the above

According to St. Paul, all immorality is the result of _____.
(a) human pride
(b) ignorance of God
(c) the design for power and riches

What was the most important role of the prophets in the Old Testament?
(a) to offer sacrifice
(b) to interpret dreams
(c) to call people to a change of heart

Answers

(c) with her prayers (par. 965)

(1 point)

False (par. 1501)

(2 points)

(c) the Christian family (par. 2205)

(2 points)

(a) Jesus is Lord (par. 2670)

(2 points)

Questions

How did Mary help the early Church?
(a) with her miracles
(b) with her preaching
(c) with her prayers

Terminal illness always leads to anguish and despair.

True or false?

Which of these is a sign of the communion between the Father and the Son and the Holy Spirit?
(a) creation
(b) church law
(c) the Christian family

"No one can say, _____, except by the Holy Spirit." (1Cor 12:3)
(a) Jesus is Lord
(b) the Our Father
(c) thy will be done

Answers

(c) by worshipping the golden calf (par. 210)

(2 points)

(a) Baptism (par. 1213)

(2 points)

False (par. 2068)

(2 points)

False (par. 2603)

(1 point)

Questions

How were the Israelites unfaithful to God during the time of Moses?

(a) by complaining
(b) by returning to Egypt
(c) by worshipping the golden calf

What sacrament is called the "door" to the other sacraments?

(a) Baptism
(b) Eucharist
(c) Matrimony

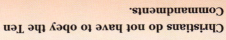

**Christians do not have to obey the Ten Commandments.
True or false?**

**Sometimes in prayer Jesus decided differently from his Father's will.
True or false?**

Answers

(b) souls in purgatory (par. 954)

(2 points)

False (par. 1508)

(2 points)

(b) a long life (Ex 20:12)

(2 points)

(b) Lamb of God (par. 2665)

(2 points)

Questions

Who belongs to the Church besides pilgrims on earth and saints in heaven?
(a) pagans
(b) souls in purgatory
(c) fallen angels

All Christians have a special charism of healing.

True or false?

"Honor your father and your mother, that you may have _____."
(a) a good inheritance
(b) a long life
(c) peace of mind

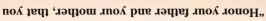

"_____ who takes away the sin of the world, have mercy on us."
(a) Lord God
(b) Lamb of God
(c) Son of God

Answers

False (par. 183)

(2 points)

(c) the chair (par. 1184)

(2 points)

True (par. 1850)

(1 point)

(a) the boy Jesus (par. 2599)

(2 points)

Questions

Faith is important, but not necessary for salvation.
True or false?

From where does the priest lead community worship?

(a) the ambo
(b) the altar
(c) the chair

According to St. Augustine, it is sinful to love yourself more than God.
True or false?

Who said in Lk 2:49, "I must be in my Father's house?"

(a) the boy Jesus
(b) Elijah the prophet
(c) John the Baptist

Answers

(a) hermits (par. 921)

(3 points)

(b) satisfaction (par. 1459)

(2 points)

(a) first (par. 2174)

(1 point)

(b) praise (par. 2639)

(3 points)

Questions

Whose life is considered a "silent preaching of the Lord?"
(a) hermits
(b) priests
(c) laity

What is another word for penance?
(a) consolation
(b) satisfaction
(c) Lent

Jesus rose from the dead "on the _____ day of the week."
(a) first
(b) third
(c) last

What form of prayer expresses most immediately that God is God?
(a) petition
(b) praise
(c) intercession

Answers

(b) supernatural (par. 179)

(2 points)

False (par. 1179)

(1 point)

(b) fifth commandment (par. 2073)

(3 points)

(b) he was asked to sacrifice his only son (par. 2572)

(2 points)

Questions

Faith is a ———— gift from God.
(a) merited
(b) supernatural
(c) natural

According to Church law, worship can only happen in a church.
True or false?

Which commandment forbids abusive language?
(a) fourth commandment
(b) fifth commandment
(c) sixth commandment

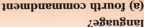

How was Abraham's faith put to the test?
(a) his wife turned to a pillar of salt
(b) he was asked to sacrifice his only son
(c) he grew old before he reached the promised land

Answers

(b) laity (par. 897)

(2 points)

(d) all the above (par. 1460)

(2 points)

(a) the Sabbath (par. 2172)

(2 points)

False (par. 2653)

(1 point)

Questions

What does the Church call baptized individuals who are not ordained?
(a) catechumens
(b) laity
(c) pagans

Which of these is a form of penance?
(a) prayer
(b) works of mercy
(c) giving alms
(d) all the above

What is a "day of protest" against the servitude of work?
(a) the Sabbath
(b) Labor Day
(c) May Day

The Church does not encourage private reading of the Sacred Scriptures. True or false?

Answers

False (par. 160)

(2 points)

(b) Easter (par. 1169)

(2 points)

(b) 7 (par. 1831)

(2 points)

(a) the Lord is my God (par. 2582)

(3 points)

Questions

God leads people in a way that they cannot refuse to follow.
True or false?

According to St. Athanasius, what feast is called "the Great Sunday?"
(a) Christmas
(b) Easter
(c) Pentecost

There are how many gifts of the Holy Spirit?
(a) 3
(b) 7
(c) 10

What does the name "Elijah" mean?
(a) the Lord is my God
(b) God is with us
(c) God saves his people

Answers

(a) Peter (par. 881)

(1 point)

False (par. 1457)

(1 point)

(b) the Sabbath (par. 2171)

(1 point)

(c) thanks (par. 2638)

(2 points)

Questions

Who did Jesus name the "rock" of the Church?
(a) Peter
(b) Judas
(c) Joseph

Children should receive First Communion before they go to First Confession.
True or false?

Which of these is a sign of God's covenant?
(a) lightening and thunder
(b) the Sabbath
(c) the sun

"In all circumstances, give _____, for this is the will of God for you in Christ Jesus."
(1Thes 5:18)
(a) alms
(b) a listening ear
(c) thanks

Answers

(c) her faith (par. 148)

(1 point)

(b) feast days (par. 1164)

(2 points)

False (par. 1804)

(1 point)

(c) the Temple of Jerusalem (par. 2580)

(2 points)

Questions

What helped Mary to accept becoming the mother of Jesus?
(a) her personality
(b) her relationship to Joseph
(c) her faith

Days of the year that recall the wonderful saving actions of God are called _____.
(a) recollection days
(b) feast days
(c) ember days

It is not necessary to work at being good. True or false?

What is called the house of prayer in Israel?
(a) the soul
(b) the ark of the covenant
(c) the Temple of Jerusalem

Answers

(c) the Apostles (par. 860)

(2 points)

False (par. 1458)

(2 points)

False (par. 2132)

(1 point)

(b) Eucharist (par. 2643)

(3 points)

Questions

Who are considered the foundation stones of the Church?
(a) Adam and Eve
(b) Joseph and Mary
(c) the Apostles

Only those who commit mortal sin should go to confession.
True or false?

It is against the first commandment to venerate statues or sacred images.
True or false?

What is called the sacrifice of praise?
(a) Baptism
(b) Eucharist
(c) the Friday fast

Answers

(c) the Holy Spirit (par. 152)

(2 points)

False (par. 1121)

(2 points)

(c) God (par. 1803)

(3 points)

(a) Jonah and the flood

(1 point)

Questions

What helps us to realize that Jesus is Lord?
(a) our desire that it be so
(b) our intelligence
(c) the Holy Spirit

All the sacraments give a special sacramental seal.
True or false?

St. Gregory of Nyssa once said, "The goal of the virtuous life is to become like _____."
(a) the virgin Mary
(b) a saint
(c) God

What two do not go together?
(a) Jonah and the flood
(b) David and the Psalms
(c) Solomon and the Temple

Answers

(c) the Holy Spirit (par. 852)

(1 point)

(b) deceive (1Jn 1:8)

(2 points)

(a) the first commandment (par. 2112)

(2 points)

(c) consecrated (par. 2687)

(2 points)

Questions

Who leads the mission of the Church?
(a) missionaries
(b) bishops
(c) the Holy Spirit

"If we say we are without sin, we _____ ourselves."
(a) are true to
(b) deceive
(c) betray

Which commandment forbids giving one's whole life to something other than the one true God?
(a) the first commandment
(b) the second commandment
(c) the third commandment

Priests, monks and nuns live a _____ life.
(a) sinless
(b) married
(c) consecrated

Answers

(c) God (par. 198)

(1 point)

(a) the ordained (par. 1119)

(2 points)

(a) blasphemy (par. 2162)

(2 point)

(c) Jacob (par. 2573)

(2 points)

Questions

Which is the beginning and end of everything?
(a) heaven
(b) the universe
(c) God

Who are appointed "to nourish the Church with the Word and grace of God?"
(a) the ordained
(b) the laity
(c) the nuns
(d) all the above

It can be the sin of _____ to make fun of the Virgin Mary and the saints.
(a) blasphemy
(b) idolatry
(c) bigotry

Who in the Old Testament fathered twelve sons who eventually became the twelve tribes of Israel?
(a) Abraham
(b) Isaac
(c) Jacob

Answers

False (par. 841, 851)

(2 points)

(b) love the poor (par. 1397)

(1 point)

False (par. 2104)

(1 point)

(c) groaning (par. 2630)

(3 points)

Questions

God's plan of salvation only includes Christians.
True or false?

The Eucharist helps us to _____.
(a) be successful
(b) love the poor
(c) stay healthy

Seeking the truth keeps Christians from truly respecting different religions.
True or false?

What does St. Paul call prayer of petition?
(a) praising
(b) running
(c) groaning

Answers

(a) Sacred Scripture (par. 81)

(2 points)

(b) sacraments (par. 1116)

(2 points)

(a) people sharing their talents (par. 1937)

(1 point)

(c) Jacob (Gn 27:1-45)

(3 points)

Questions

What is the speech of God?
(a) Sacred Scripture
(b) thunder and lightening
(c) silence

Which are the masterworks of God in the Church today?
(a) miracles
(b) sacraments
(c) relics

What helps societies grow and develop?
(a) people sharing their talents
(b) people living in common
(c) people minding their own business

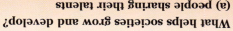

Which patriarch tricked his older brother out of his birthright?
(a) Abraham
(b) Isaac
(c) Jacob

Answers

(c) our racial differences (par. 791)

(2 points)

(a) not worthy (par. 1386)

(2 points)

(a) complacency (par. 1784)

(2 points)

False (par. 2636)

(1 point)

Questions

What does not matter before God?
(a) our sins
(b) our beliefs
(c) our racial differences

"Lord, I am _____ to receive you, but only say the word and my soul shall be healed."
(a) not worthy
(b) blessed
(c) amazed

What is an obstacle to a good conscience?
(a) complacency
(b) public education
(c) guilt

There are people even Christian prayer cannot help.
True or false?

Answers

(c) Israel (par. 751)

(1 point)

(c) incense and Anointing of the Sick

(1 point)

(c) to be a neighbor to others (par. 1932)

(1 point)

True (par. 2570) (Gn 15:2)

(2 points)

Questions

Which was called the "holy people of God?"
(a) Egypt
(b) the Roman Empire
(c) Israel

What does not go together?
(a) water and Baptism
(b) oil and Confirmation
(c) incense and Anointing of the Sick

What is every person's duty in society?
(a) to seek power
(b) to question authority
(c) to be a neighbor to others

When Abraham first prays in words, he complains to God.
True or false?

Answers

(b) by helping the poor and suffering (par. 544)

(1 point)

(c) our faith (par. 1381)

(2 points)

False (par. 2059)

(1 point)

(a) the kingdom of God (par. 2632)

(1 point)

Questions

How can we best serve Jesus?
(a) by getting the best grades in class
(b) by helping the poor and suffering
(c) by doing what we want

What allows us to see Jesus present in the Eucharist?
(a) our senses
(b) our imagination
(c) our faith

Moses was responsible for writing the Ten Commandments. True or false?

What did Jesus tell us to seek first before everything else?
(a) the Kingdom of God
(b) peace on earth
(c) manna from heaven

Answers

False (par. 55)

(2 points)

(d) all the above (par. 1088)

(3 points)

(b) respect for the dignity of people (par. 1929)

(2 points)

False (par. 2570)

(1 point)

Questions

The sin of Adam and Eve destroyed any relationship we have with God.
True or false?

How is Jesus present and active in the Church today?
(a) through the sacraments
(b) in prayer groups
(c) through the Scriptures
(d) all the above

What is essential in a just society?
(a) strong leaders controlling the masses
(b) respect for the dignity of people
(c) everyone agreeing with one another
(d) all the above

Words are more important than actions in our life of prayer.
True or false?

Answers

(c) charity (par. 815)

(2 points)

True (par. 1371)

(1 point)

(c) false witness (par. 2464)

(2 points)

(b) the centurion (par. 2610)

(2 points)

Questions

Above all, what bond of unity keeps the Church together?
(a) the ecumenical dialogue
(b) the Pope
(c) charity

The Mass helps those who have died. True or false?

"You shall not bear _____ against your neighbor."
(a) arms
(b) a grudge
(c) false witness

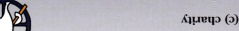

Who said the words: "O Lord, I am not worthy to have you enter under my roof. . ." (Mt 8:8)
(a) the woman in hemorrhage
(b) the centurion
(c) Zacchaeus

Answers

False (par. 41)

(2 points)

(d) all the above (par. 1070)

(2 points)

(a) cooperation and friendship between people (par. 1939)

(2 points)

(a) he walked with God (Gn 6:9)

(2 points)

Questions

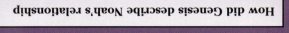

Not all creatures can reflect what God is like. True or false?

In the New Testament, liturgy means _____.
(a) worship of God
(b) proclamation of the Gospel
(c) active charity
(d) all the above

What is meant by human solidarity?
(a) cooperation and friendship between people
(b) people achieving personal goals
(c) rich people taking advantage of poor people

How did Genesis describe Noah's relationship to God?
(a) he walked with God
(b) he ran from God
(c) he feared God

Answers

(b) the Church (par. 805)

(1 point)

True (par. 1368)

(2 points)

(a) the name (par. 2142-2143)

(1 point)

(b) the tax collector (par. 2631)

(3 points)

Questions

Which of these is called the "Body of Christ"?
(a) the Pope
(b) the Church
(c) the Bible

The Eucharist gives our lives new value each time we celebrate it.
True or false?

"You shall not take _____ of the Lord your God in vain."
(a) the name
(b) the land
(c) the law

Who said the words: "O God, be merciful to me a sinner?" (Lk 18:13)
(a) the blind man
(b) the tax collector
(c) the rich young man

Answers

(a) the world's order and beauty (par. 32)

(2 points)

(c) rising (par. 1067)

(1 point)

(a) to be responsible for their actions
   (par. 1781)

(2 points)

(c) a mysterious encounter (par. 2567)

(1 point)

Questions

What else helps us to know about God besides faith?
(a) the world's order and beauty
(b) the sinfulness of humanity
(c) the news

"Dying he destroyed our death, _____ he restored our life."
(a) living
(b) forgiving
(c) rising

Conscience always enables people _____.
(a) to be responsible for their actions
(b) to choose the correct behavior
(c) to have peace of mind following any decision

Prayer is like _____.
(a) running after idols
(b) making believe
(c) a mysterious encounter
(d) all the above

Answers

(c) to be a light to the world (par. 782)

(2 points)

(c) the bread and wine (par. 1333)

(2 points)

(c) strange gods (par. 2084)

(1 point)

(b) greatness (par. 2619)

(2 points)

Questions

What is the mission of God's people?
(a) to raise money
(b) to achieve world peace
(c) to be a light to the world

What is the "work of human hands" offered to God at Mass?
(a) money for the poor
(b) the prayers and songs of the people
(c) the bread and wine

"I am the Lord your God; you shall not have _____ before me."
(a) false witnesses
(b) power and riches
(c) strange gods

"My soul proclaims the _____ of the Lord; my spirit rejoices in God my savior." (Lk 1:46-47)
(a) power
(b) greatness
(c) glory

Answers

(b) love   (par. 25)

(3 points)

False   (par. 1143)

(2 points)

False   (par. 1742)

(2 points)

True   (par. 2566)

(3 points)

Questions

What is the supreme goal of everything that the Church teaches and believes?
(a) peace on earth
(b) love
(c) freedom from suffering

Only the ordained can serve as lectors and acolytes.
True or false?

Christians are not as free as other people because of all the commandments to follow.
True or false?

Humanity lost its likeness to God through sin.
True or false?

Answers

(c) 12 (par. 765)

(2 points)

(b) Confirmation (par. 1309)

(2 points)

False (par. 2007)

(2 points)

(d) all the above (par. 2629)

(2 points)

Questions

How many tribes made up the nation of Israel?
(a) 7
(b) 10
(c) 12

What sacrament gives one a special sense of belonging to the universal Church?
(a) Matrimony
(b) Confirmation
(c) Anointing of the Sick

Because God has created us, we deserve to be with him in heaven. True or false?

What kind of prayer is a turning back to God?
(a) prayer of contrition
(b) prayer of lamentation
(c) prayer of petition
(d) all the above

Answers

(b) catechesis (par. 4)

(2 points)

(c) laying on of hands (par. 1597)

(2 points)

(b) is honest about personal weakness or sin (par. 1783-1784)

(2 points)

(a) it is communion with Christ (par. 2565)

(1 point)

Questions

The Church's effort to teach people about Jesus is called _____.
(a) revelation
(b) catechesis
(c) indoctrination

What is the most important action in the sacrament of Holy Orders?
(a) anointing with oil
(b) presentation of the chalice and paten
(c) laying on of hands

A person with a well formed conscience _____.
(a) blames others for mistakes
(b) is honest about personal weakness or sin
(c) never commits sin

Why is prayer "Christian?"
(a) it is communion with Christ
(b) it was first taught by Jesus
(c) it can only be done properly by Christians

Answers

(b) the Son (par. 679, 682)

(3 points)

(a) the forehead (par. 1300)

(2 points)

False (par. 2005)

(2 points)

False (par. 2629)

(1 point)

Questions

We can pray without even being aware of our relationship to God.
True or false?

We can know for sure that we will be saved.
True or false?

Where is a person anointed during Confirmation?
(a) the forehead
(b) the hands
(c) the heart
(d) all the above

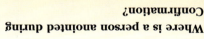

Who will judge the whole world?
(a) the Father
(b) the Son
(c) the Holy Spirit

Answers

(a) receiving the inheritance of everlasting life (par. 1)

(2 points)

False (par. 1576)

(2 points)

(c) the Word of God (par. 1785)

(1 point)

(a) a response to (par. 2561)

(1 point)

Questions

What benefit is there to becoming adopted children of God?
(a) receiving the inheritance of everlasting life
(b) receiving promised land
(c) receiving whatever we ask for in prayer

Only the Pope can ordain bishops. True or false?

What helps form a good conscience?
(a) a sinful life
(b) following the crowd
(c) the Word of God

Our prayer of petition is _____ God's promises to us.
(a) a response to
(b) a thanksgiving for
(c) a settlement of

Answers

(c) by his Resurrection (par. 654)

(2 points)

(a) Holy Thrusday (par. 1297)

(3 points)

(b) evangelical counsels (par. 1973)

(3 points)

(c) supplication (par. 2629)

(3 points)

Questions

How did Jesus "open for us the way to a new life?"
(a) by his birth
(b) by his baptism
(c) by his Resurrection

When is the oil for Confirmation blessed?
(a) Palm Sunday
(b) Holy Thursday
(c) Good Friday

What do we call the three vows of poverty, chastity and obedience?
(a) spiritual works of mercy
(b) evangelical counsels
(c) moral virtues

What is prayer of petition sometimes called?
(a) lamentation
(b) praise
(c) supplication

Answers

(b) Herod (Mt 2:16-19)

(2 points)

(b) servants (Mk 10:43)

(1 point)

(b) human fulfillment is found in the love of God (par. 1718-1721)

(2 points)

(a) God's desire for us (par. 2560)

(2 points)

Questions

Who wanted to make sure that the Messiah would not survive?
(a) Pontius Pilate
(b) Herod
(c) Caesar Augustus

Jesus told his disciples that in order to be great they must become _____.
(a) good speakers
(b) servants
(c) effective faith healers

What is the central message of the Beatitudes?
(a) work hard and you will prosper
(b) human fulfillment is found in the love of God
(c) avoid fighting at all costs

What comes first?
(a) God's desire for us
(b) our desire for God
(c) God's need to have us respond

Answers

(a) by sharing a meal with them (par. 645)

(2 points)

(a) myron (par. 1289)

(3 points)

(c) love (par. 1974)

(2 points)

(c) always obey God's will (par. 2677)

(1 point)

Questions

How did the risen Jesus show his disciples that he was not a ghost?
(a) by sharing a meal with them
(b) by appearing as a gardener
(c) by performing a miracle

What is another word for chrism oil?
(a) myron
(b) oil of the sick
(c) oil of catechumen

Which of these has been called the queen of all virtues?
(a) faith
(b) hope
(c) love

How can we best imitate the virgin Mary?
(a) never get married
(b) go to church often
(c) always obey God's will

Answers

(b) Adam and Eve's choice to disobey God (par. 390-391)

(2 points)

(c) a holy priesthood (par. 1546)

(1 point)

(b) hope (par. 1817)

(2 points)

(a) a personal relationship with God (par. 2558)

(2 points)

Questions

What is meant by the "fall of humanity?"
(a) Adam and Eve's choice to hide from God
(b) Adam and Eve's choice to disobey God
(c) Adam and Eve being bitten by a snake

Through Baptism and Confirmation, Christians are "consecrated to be _____."
(a) better than anyone else
(b) perfect in every way
(c) a holy priesthood

Which virtue helps a person desire God's kingdom?
(a) faith
(b) hope
(c) fortitude

How is prayer best described?
(a) a personal relationship with God
(b) quiet time during the day
(c) special words addressed to God

Answers

False (par. 618)

(1 point)

(b) by the laying on of hands (par. 1288)

(2 points)

(b) laws (Heb 8:10)

(2 points)

(b) his great faith (par. 2610)

(2 points)

Questions

Jesus promised his disciples that they would never have to suffer. True or false?

How did the apostles give the gift of the Holy Spirit to the newly baptized?
(a) by forgiving their sins
(b) by the laying on of hands
(c) by the greeting of peace

The Lord said to the nation of Israel, "I will put my _____ into their minds, and write them on their hearts."
(a) beatitudes
(b) laws
(c) beliefs

What amazed Jesus about the Roman centurion?
(a) his power
(b) his great faith
(c) his political connections

Answers

(b) holy (par. 374)

(2 points)

(a) the full outpouring of the Holy Spirit (par. 1302)

(2 points)

(a) justice (par. 1807)

(2 points)

(a) the Apostles' Creed (par. 2558)

(2 points)

Questions

What was the original condition of the first human beings?
(a) sinful
(b) holy
(c) confused

What is the most important effect of the sacrament of Confirmation?
(a) the full outpouring of the Holy Spirit
(b) the ability to avoid the near occasion of sin
(c) the ability to preach Christ

Which virtue helps people to act in the fairest way toward their neighbor?
(a) justice
(b) fortitude
(c) prudence

Through what prayer does the Church profess its faith?
(a) the Apostles' Creed
(b) the Ten Commandments
(c) the Acts of the Apostles

Answers

False (par. 609)

(2 points)

(a) Easter (par. 1287)

(3 points)

False (par. 1930)

(2 points)

(b) because our prayer is based on Jesus' prayer (par. 2614)

(2 points)

Questions

Jesus had no choice but to give his life to save the world.
True or false?

When did Jesus first give the gift of the Holy Spirit to his followers?

(a) Easter
(b) Pentecost
(c) Ascension

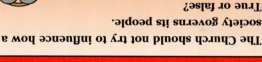

The Church should not try to influence how a society governs its people.
True or false?

Why do we know our prayers will always be heard?

(a) because we are sincere
(b) because our prayer is based on Jesus' prayer
(c) because our needs are great

Answers

(c) the Nicene Creed (par. 190)

(2 points)

**(b) immersion in or pouring of water
   (par. 1239)**

(1 point)

False (par. 1753)

(2 points)

False (par. 2726)

(2 points)

Questions

What prayer mentions the persons of the Blessed Trinity?
(a) the Our Father
(b) the Act of Contrition
(c) the Nicene Creed

What is the most important action of Baptism?
(a) anointing with oil
(b) immersion in or pouring of water
(c) lighting of the candle

A person may commit a sin if it will help others.
True or false?

Christians must learn to pray alone, without any help from God.
True or false?

Answers

(a) Redemption (par. 517)

(3 points)

False (par. 1287)

(2 points)

(b) grace (par. 1889)

(1 point)

(c) ask the Father in Jesus' name (par. 2614)

(1 point)

Questions

What is meant by Jesus giving his whole life to save us?
(a) Redemption
(b) Resurrection
(c) Revelation

Only Jesus is blessed with the fullness of the Holy Spirit.

True or false?

What most helps a person decide how to choose between good and evil?
(a) intelligence
(b) grace
(c) temptation

What does Jesus teach us to do in prayer?
(a) always pray alone
(b) don't use memorized prayers
(c) ask the Father in Jesus' name

Answers

(b) at Baptism (par. 265)

(1 point)

(a) Baptism (par. 1226)

(2 points)

(b) treating others unfairly because of their ethnic background (par. 1935-1938)

(2 points)

(c) persevere (par. 2728)

(2 points)

Questions

When do we first begin to share in the life of grace?
(a) at birth
(b) at Baptism
(c) at Reconciliation

What sacrament is always associated with faith?
(a) Baptism
(b) Marriage
(c) Anointing of the Sick

What is an example of prejudice?
(a) interracial marriage
(b) treating others unfairly because of their ethnic background
(c) going to a private school to get a better education

When God does not seem to answer our prayers, what should we do?
(a) give up
(b) ask in a different way
(c) persevere

Answers

(b) the Son (par. 443-444)

(2 points)

(b) at his baptism (Mt 3:13-17)

(2 points)

False (par. 1869)

(1 point)

(c) "Father, forgive them, for they know not what they do" (par. 2605)

(2 points)

Questions

What title of Jesus suggests his divinity?
(a) the Good Shepherd
(b) the Son
(c) the Prophet

When did God first reveal publicly that Jesus was his beloved son?
(a) at his birth
(b) at his baptism
(c) at his resurrection

Personal sins have no effect on our neighbors. True or false?

What was Jesus' prayer on the cross?
(a) "Let this cup pass from me"
(b) "Turn the other cheek"
(c) "Father, forgive them, for they know not what they do"